LOVE SUCKS

LOVE SUCKS

BY DARIA SUMMERS

ILLUSTRATIONS BY EMMA MUNGER

Smith Street Books

LOVE, WE'RE TOLD by sages and poets, by artists and activists, is the answer. Love will set us free. It will lift us up when we're down, give us hope when we're hopeless, give our very lives the meaning and purpose we crave. We hear it so much it's become a sort of everlasting refrain. All you need is love. Love is all you need.

Bullshit. Love will not – in any true or lasting way – set you free. It can't pay your bills when you're broke. People who are in love seem to become at least 10 per cent dumber. And if love really is the answer, could you please rephrase the question?

Love, it seems, is a collective delusion propped up by an effective marketing plan. A lie perpetuated by poets. The great rock 'n' roll swindle. The greatest trick the devil ever pulled was probably the invention of Valentine's Day.

You want a truth that's universally acknowledged? Love sucks. It is the actual worst. It'll make you feel things for people, and then those people will leave. It's like a drug, but instead of making you cool, it just makes you cry over soppy ads on TV. It will make you earnest. And it will make you boring. And it will end.

If there's one thing that both sceptics and converts can agree on, it's that love is mysterious. Is it the universal life force or just chemicals whizzing around your body that make you do a bunch of dumb things? No offence, lovers, but we're betting on the latter.

'Love,' said Charles Bukowski, 'is a dog from Hell.' We'd like to add that it will probably give you rabies. So let's hear it for the cynics and the heart-bored and to anyone who's ever looked love in the eye and thought: meh. This one's for you.

LOVE SUCKS

sometimes it

FEELS GOOD

sometimes it's just another way to

Bleed

LAURELL K. HAMILTON
BLUE MOON

To my secret

I think only stupid people have good relationships

ENID
GHOST WORLD

WE ARE ALL MORE INTELLIGENT THAN WE ARE CAPABLE, AND AWARENESS OF THE INSANITY OF LOVE HAS NEVER SAVED ANYONE FROM THE DISEASE

ALAIN DE BOTTON
ON LOVE

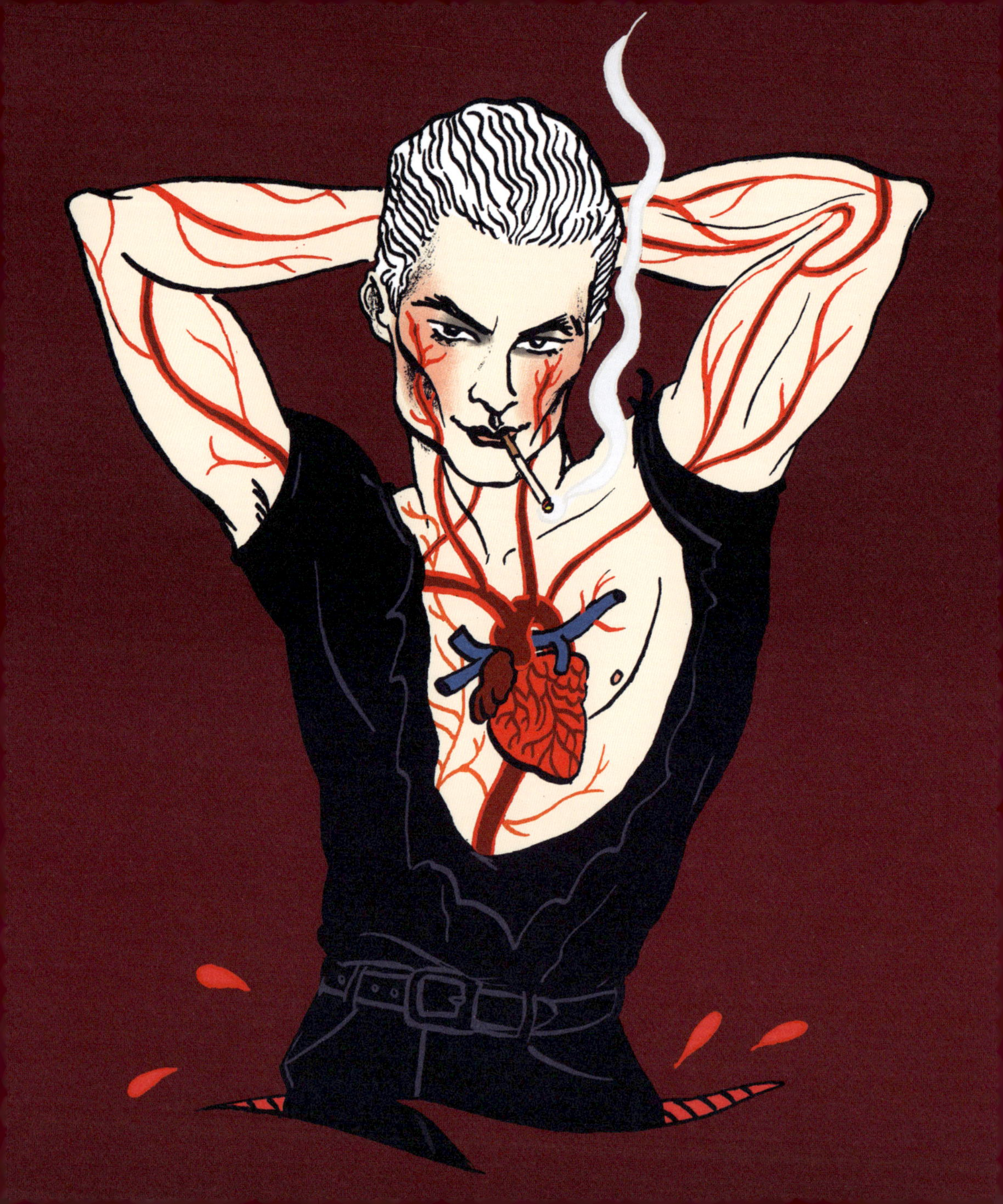

LOVE ISN'T BRAINS CHILDREN
IT'S BLOOD
BLOOD SCREAMING
INSIDE YOU TO WORK ITS WILL
I may be Love's Bitch but at least I'm man enough to admit it

SPIKE
BUFFY: THE VAMPIRE SLAYER

Love indeed – whoever invented love ought to be shot.

NANCY MITFORD
LOVE IN A COLD CLIMATE

THE FIRST DIVORCE IS THE ONLY TOUGH ONE AFTER THAT IT'S MERELY A PROBLEM OF MATHEMATICS

RAYMOND CHANDLER
THE LONG GOODBYE

YOU CAN BE MARRIED AND BORED, OR *Single* AND *Lonely*. AIN'T NO HAPPINESS NOWHERE.

CHRIS ROCK
NEVER SCARED

If you want to sacrifice the admiration of many men for the criticism of one, go ahead, get married.

KATHARINE HEPBURN

LOVE DRAINS YOU, TAKES WITH IT MUCH OF YOUR BLOOD SUGAR & WATER WEIGHT. YOU ARE LIKE A HOUSE SLOWLY LOSING ITS ELECTRICITY, THE FANS SLOWING, THE LIGHTS DIMMING AND FLICKERING; THE CLOCKS STOP AND GO AND STOP.

LORRIE MOORE
SELF-HELP

If we judge of love by the majority of its results, it rather resembles hatred than friendship.

FRANÇOIS DE LA ROCHEFOUCAULD

REFLECTIONS; OR SENTENCES AND MORAL MAXIMS

FRIENDSHIP IS A SERIOUS AFFECTION; THE MOST SUBLIME OF ALL AFFECTIONS, BECAUSE IT IS FOUNDED ON PRINCIPLE AND CEMENTED BY TIME. THE REVERSE MAY BE SAID OF LOVE.

MARY WOLLSTONECRAFT
A VINDICATION OF THE RIGHTS OF WOMEN

I Don't Care about ANYONE, and the Feeling is quite Obviously Mutual.

SYLVIA PLATH

THE UNABRIDGED JOURNALS OF SYLVIA PLATH

I don't believe that people would ever fall in love or want to be married if they hadn't been told about it.

IT'S LIKE ABROAD: NO ONE WOULD WANT TO GO THERE IF THEY HADN'T BEEN TOLD IT EXISTED.

EVELYN WAUGH
DECLINE AND FALL

ALCOHOL can provide a form of SUBSTITUTE for a reasonably HARMONIOUS sex life

INGE AND STEN HEGELER
AN ABZ OF LOVE

To hell with God damned 'L'Amour'. It always causes far more trouble than it is worth. Don't run after it. Don't court it. Keep it waiting off stage until you're good and ready for it and even then treat it with the suspicious disdain that it deserves.

NOËL COWARD

THE LETTERS OF NOËL COWARD

THE MOST JUST comparison of love IS THAT OF A Fever, AND WE HAVE NO power over either, AS TO ITS violence or ITS DURATION.

FRANÇOIS DE LA ROCHEFOUCAULD
REFLECTIONS; OR SENTENCES AND MORAL MAXIMS

This is what happened in love: one of you cried a lot and then both of you grew sarcastic.

LORRIE MOORE
LIKE LIFE

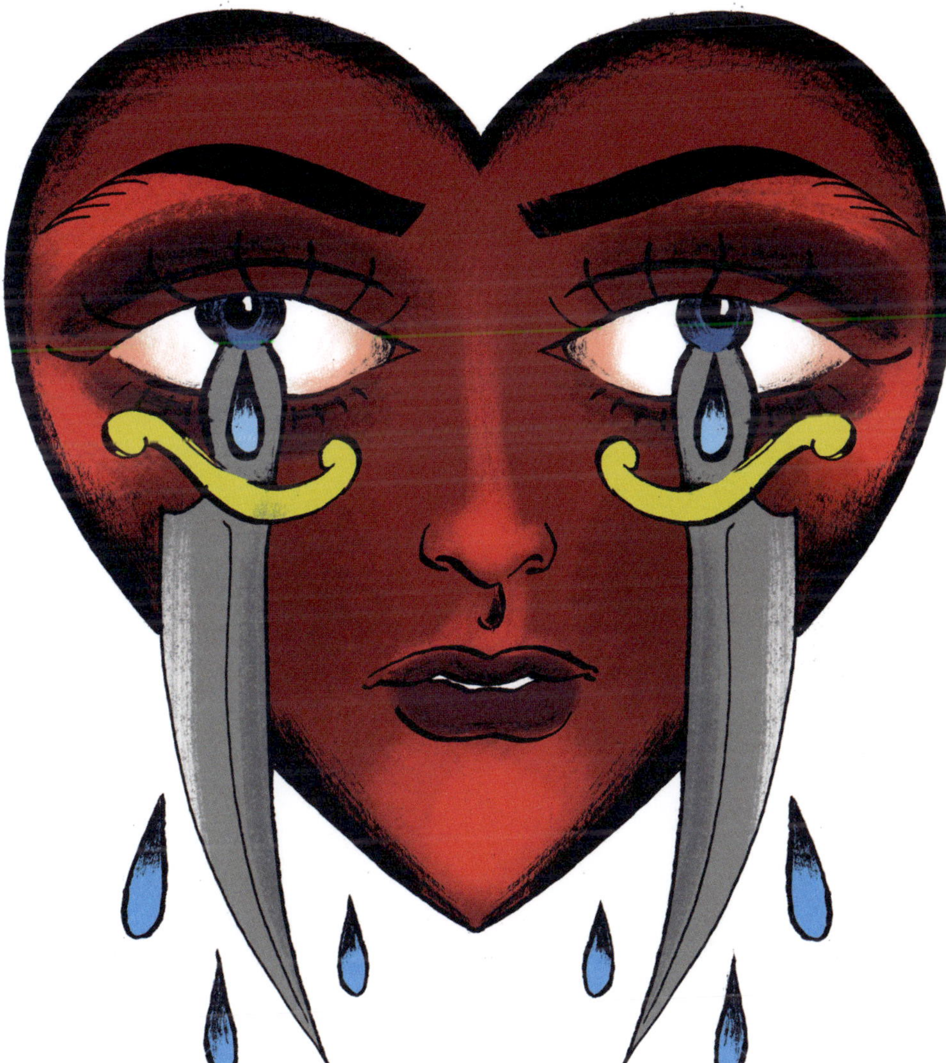

Sex alleviates tension. Love causes it.

WOODY ALLEN

TO LOVE IS TO SUFFER.
To avoid Suffering, one must
Not Love.
BUT, THEN ONE SUFFERS FROM NOT LOVING.
Therefore, to love is to suffer.
NOT TO LOVE IS TO SUFFER,
TO SUFFER IS TO SUFFER.
TO BE HAPPY IS TO LOVE,
to be happy, then, is to suffer,
But Suffering Makes One Unhappy
THEREFORE, TO BE UNHAPPY ONE MUST LOVE,
OR LOVE TO SUFFER, OR SUFFER FROM
TOO MUCH HAPPINESS –
I hope you're getting this down.

SONJA
LOVE AND DEATH

IN FAIRY TALES, THE PRINCESSES KISS THE FROGS, AND THE FROGS BECOME PRINCES.

IN REAL LIFE, THE PRINCESSES KISS PRINCES, AND THE PRINCES TURN INTO FROGS.

PAULO COELHO

BY THE RIVER PIEDRA I SAT DOWN AND WEPT

WHEN PEOPLE CLAIM TO HAVE
LOST THEIR HEART
IT'S USUALLY ONLY
THEIR WITS
THAT HAVE
VANISHED

PETER PRANGE
THE PHILOSOPHER'S KISS

Love:
A TEMPORARY insanity CURABLE BY Marriage.

AMBROSE BIERCE
THE DEVIL'S DICTIONARY

THE MOST HAPPY MARRIAGE
I CAN PICTURE OR
IMAGINE TO MYSELF
would be the
UNION
OF A
Deaf Man
TO A
blind Woman

SAMUEL TAYLOR COLERIDGE

To Do:
groceries
laundry
kiss Michael

Marriage is the MIRACLE that transforms a Kiss from a pleasure into a Duty

HELEN ROWLAND

A GUIDE TO MEN

People in love often become
EDGY, DANGEROUS
They lose their sense of
PERSPECTIVE
They lose their sense of
HUMOUR
They become nervous,
PSYCHOTIC BORES
They even become
KILLERS

CHARLES BUKOWSKI
WOMEN

HELL IS OTHER PEOPLE

JEAN-PAUL SARTRE
NO EXIT

REAL LOVE AMOUNTS
to withholding the
TRUTH,
even when you're offered
THE PERFECT OPPORTUNITY TO
HURT SOMEONE'S
feelings.

DAVID SEDARIS
DRESS YOUR FAMILY IN CORDUROY AND DENIM

LOVE INVOLVES A PECULIAR UNFATHOMABLE COMBINATION OF UNDERSTANDING AND MISUNDERSTANDING

DIANE ARBUS
THE ART OF PHOTOGRAPHY

When one is in Love, one always begins by deceiving oneself, and one always ends by deceiving others. THAT IS WHAT THE WORLD CALLS A Romance.

OSCAR WILDE

THE PICTURE OF DORIAN GRAY

by
ARGOT
BAUM

Dear Eli,
I'm in the middle
of the Ocean.
I haven't left my
room in four days.
I've never been more
lonely in my life,

and I think I'm
in love with
Margot.

RICHIE TENENBAUM
THE ROYAL TENENBAUMS

YOU KNOW HOW THEY SAY you only HURT the ones you love? WELL, IT WORKS BOTH WAYS.

CHUCK PALAHNIUK
FIGHT CLUB

Those who have had great passions often find all their lives made miserable in being cured of them.

FRANÇOIS DE LA ROCHEFOUCAULD
REFLECTIONS; OR SENTENCES AND MORAL MAXIMS

Love is just a LIE made to make you BLUE

ROY ORBISON
LOVE HURTS

IF YOU EXPECT NOTHING FROM SOMEBODY YOU ARE NEVER DISAPPOINTED

SYLVIA PLATH
THE BELL JAR

Falling in Love does not interest me

HENRY ROLLINS
IN *THE SYDNEY MORNING HERALD*

There's a club if
you'd like to go

You could meet somebody
who really loves you

So you go and you
stand on your own

And you leave on your own

And you go home and you cry

And you want to die.

THE SMITHS
HOW SOON IS NOW?

THE EXCESSES OF LOVE SOON PASS, BUT ITS INSUFFICIENCIES TORMENT US FOREVER.

MIGNON MCLAUGHLIN
THE COMPLETE NEUROTIC'S NOTEBOOK

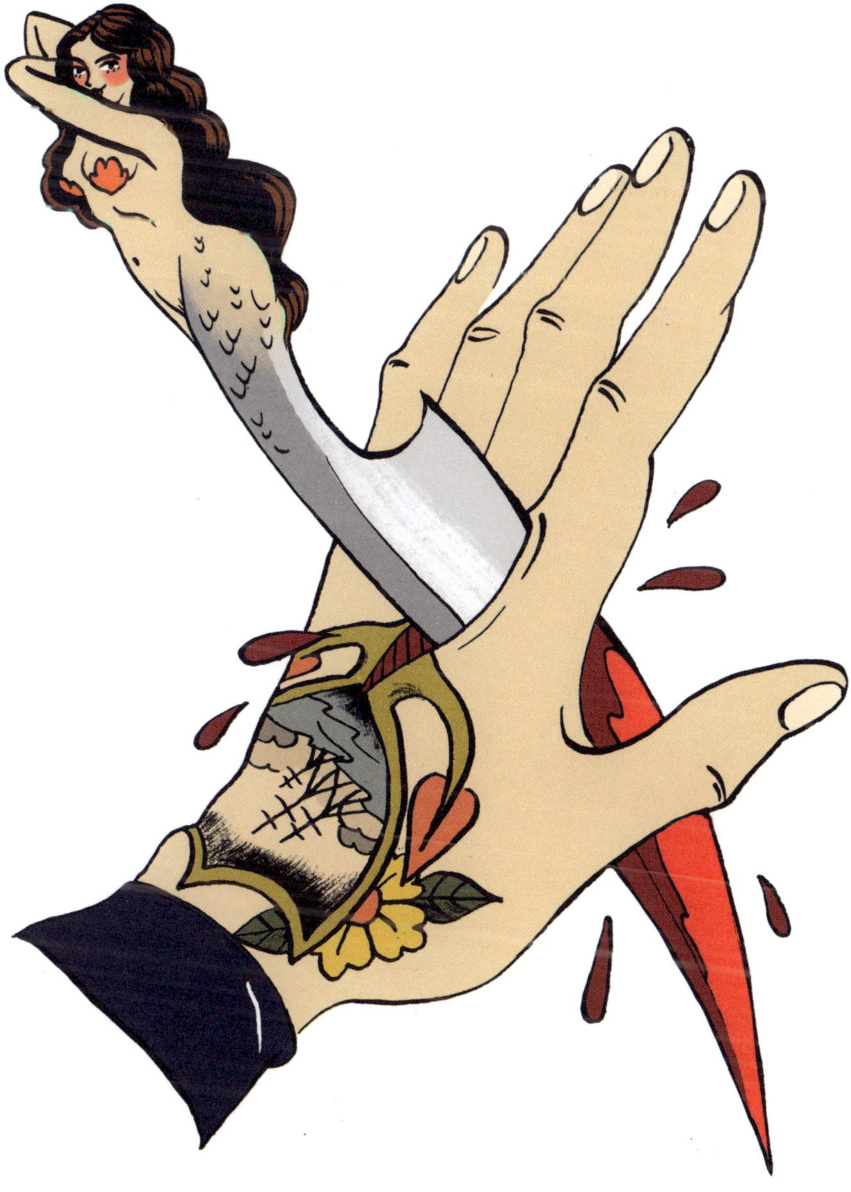

Love is a Trap.

When it appears,
We see only its light,
Not its shadows.

PAULO COELHO
BY THE RIVER PIEDRA I SAT DOWN AND WEPT

ALL PASSIONS
MAKE US
COMMIT
SOME FAULTS,
LOVE ALONE
MAKES US
RIDICULOUS.

FRANÇOIS DE LA ROCHEFOUCAULD
REFLECTIONS; OR SENTENCES AND MORAL MAXIMS

I WAS NAUSEOUS and TINGLY ALL OVER I was EITHER in LOVE OR I had SMALLPOX

WOODY ALLEN

LOVE
IS A
GRAVE
MENTAL
DISEASE

PLATO
PHAEDRUS

IF YOU LOVE SOMETHING SET IT FREE, BUT DON'T BE SURPRISED IF IT COMES BACK WITH HERPES.

CHUCK PALAHNIUK
HAUNTED

Love is a Madness

PLATO
PHAEDRUS

A WEDDING IS A FUNERAL WHERE YOU SMELL YOUR OWN FLOWERS

EDDIE CANTOR
KID MILLIONS

When we want to read of the deeds that are done for love, whither do we turn?

TO THE MURDER COLUMN

GEORGE BERNARD SHAW
THREE PLAYS FOR PURITANS

LOVE IS SOMETHING SO UGLY THAT THE HUMAN RACE WOULD DIE OUT IF LOVERS COULD SEE WHAT THEY WERE DOING.

LEONARDO DA VINCI
QUOTED IN *COLLECTED WORKS OF PAUL VALÉRY, VOLUME 8: LEONARDO, POE, MALLARME*

Love is only a dirty trick played on us to achieve continuation of the species

W. SOMERSET MAUGHAM
THE SUMMING UP

LOVE IS A FIRE
IT BURNS EVERYONE
IT DISFIGURES EVERYONE
IT IS THE WORLD'S EXCUSE
FOR BEING UGLY

LEONARD COHEN
LOVE IS A FIRE

Is it possible
to love any
Human being
without being
TORN LIMB
from LIMB?

CYRIL CONNOLLY
THE UNQUIET GRAVE: A WORD CYCLE BY PALINURUS

BEING IN LOVE means BEING WILLING to RUIN YOURSELF for the Other person

SUSAN SONTAG

AS CONSCIOUSNESS IS HARNESSED TO FLESH: JOURNALS AND NOTEBOOKS, 1964–1980

LOVE CAN CHANGE A PERSON THE WAY A PARENT CAN CHANGE A BABY—

awkwardly,

AND OFTEN WITH A GREAT DEAL OF

mess.

LEMONY SNICKET

HORSERADISH: BITTER TRUTHS YOU CAN'T AVOID

Love is the triumph of imagination over intelligence

H. L. MENCKEN

SETTLE.
BECAUSE OTHERWISE YOU'RE JUST GONNA GET OLDER AND HARDER, AND MORE ALONE.

And you're gonna do everything you can to fill that HOLE, with FRIENDS, and YOUR CAREER, and MEANINGLESS SEX, but the HOLE DOESN'T GET FILLED.

ONE DAY,
YOU'RE GONNA LOOK AROUND AND YOU'RE GOING TO REALISE THAT EVERYBODY LOVES YOU, BUT NOBODY LIKES YOU. AND THAT IS THE LONELIEST FEELING IN THE WORLD.

BOJACK HORSEMAN
BOJACK HORSEMAN

Beware of enthusiasm and of love, both are temporary and quick to sway.

ARTHUR RIMBAUD
I'M NOT THERE

LOVE IS the SELF-DELUSION we manufacture to JUSTIFY the TROUBLE we take to have SEX.

DANIEL S. GREENBERG
EXES

NO ONE HAS EVER LOVED ANYONE THE WAY EVERYONE WANTS TO BE LOVED

MIGNON MCLAUGHLIN

THE COMPLETE NEUROTIC'S NOTEBOOK

Love is a promise delivered already broken

STEVE MARTIN

Love is POISON. A sweet poison, yes, BUT IT WILL Kill YOU all the same.

GEORGE RR MARTIN
A CLASH OF KINGS

A Kiss may R·U·I·N a human life.

OSCAR WILDE
A WOMAN OF NO IMPORTANCE

JUST BEING ALIVE IS SO MUCH WORK... AFTER BEING ALIVE, THE NEXT HARDEST WORK IS HAVING SEX

ANDY WARHOL
THE PHILOSOPHY OF ANDY WARHOL

Oh, because FALLING IN LOVE turns you into an IMMEDIATE BORE. And it's DREADFUL.

GERMAINE GREER
ON *ENOUGH ROPE WITH ANDREW DENTON*

LOVE IN ACTION IS A HARSH AND DREADFUL THING COMPARED WITH LOVE IN DREAMS

FYODOR DOSTOEVSKY
THE BROTHERS KARAMAZOV

'LOVERS'... THAT WORD BUMS ME OUT UNLESS IT'S BETWEEN 'MEAT' AND 'PIZZA'

LIZ LEMON
30 ROCK

Love, love, love –
all the wretched cant of it,
masking egotism, lust, masochism,
fantasy under a mythology of
sentimental postures, a welter of
self-induced miseries and joys,
blinding and masking the essential
personalities in the frozen gestures of
courtship, in the kissing and the
dating and the desire,
the compliments and the quarrels
which vivify its barrenness.

GERMAINE GREER
THE FEMALE EUNUCH

Love is being stupid together

PAUL VALÉRY

IF
THERE ARE
JUNK YARDS
IN
H·E·L·L
love is the DOG
THAT
GUARDS THE GATES

CHARLES BUKOWSKI
LOVE IS A DOG FROM HELL

the pain of love is the pain of being alive. it is a perpetual wound.

MAUREEN DUFFY

YOU
SUCK
EM.

Smith Street Books

Published in 2018 by Smith Street Books
Melbourne | Australia
smithstreetbooks.com

ISBN: 978-192541869-9

CIP data is available from the National Library of Australia

Publisher: Hannah Koelmeyer
Compiled by: Nadia Bailey
Design: Astred Hicks
Illustrator: Emma Munger

Printed & bound in China by C&C Offset Printing Co., Ltd.
Book 46
10 9 8 7 6 5 4 3 2 1

While every effort has been made to ensure the accuracy of the quotes and their attribution, imperfection is as inevitable as heartbreak.